THE WALTZ OF THE SHADOWS
Second Edition

To my dear friend
With gratitude
and affection
Magda Herzberger
April 16, 2006

THE WALTZ OF THE SHADOWS
Second Edition

Magda Herzberger

Austin, Texas

The Waltz of the Shadows
Second Edition
By Magda Herzberger
© 2006 Magda Herzberger
The Waltz of the Shadows
Second Edition

1st World Library
DBA Groundbreaking Press
8305 Arboles Circle
Austin, TX 78737
512-657-8780
www.groundbreaking.com

Library of Congress Control Number:
ISBN: 0-9777795-0-5

Second Edition

Senior Editor
Barbara Foley

Cover Production
M. Kevin Ford

Interior Production
Brad Fregger
Tim Spivey

Dedicated to

my beloved Husband

and Family

and

in the memory of my Father,

to all those I loved and lost,

to all the innocent victums,

silenced forever,

by the Nazis

AUTHOR'S PREFACE TO SECOND EDITION

After all these years the shadows of the Holocaust are still haunting me. Often they invade my mind quite unexpectedly and dance around me "the mad waltz of memory." They are the representatives and reminders of the suffering and misery I endured as a captive 18-year-old girl in the concentration camps of Germany during World War II.

The Waltz of the Shadows is one of my first books—written in poetry—relating my experiences in the three death camps of Auschwitz, Bremen, and Bergen-Belsen. It was published in 1983 by the Philosophical Library in New York. The book also contained one of my very first prayers and musical compositions.

Many copies of *The Waltz of the Shadows* were distributed to the public through the years; the book was widely read and very much liked. The Philosophical Library went out of business and as a result, my book is out of print.

After the recent publication of *Survival*—a very detailed autobiography, covering my childhood years and my experiences in the death camps—there has been renewed interest in *The Waltz of the Shadows*. In view of this, my publisher, Mr. Brad Fregger of 1st World Library, Austin, Texas, suggested printing a second edition of the book. In this new edition, scores of two of my other musical compositions are included, along with their lyrics: *Prayer for Assistance* and *Requiem*, which was composed in memory of all the victims of the Holocaust.

Magda Herzberger
January, 2006

PUBLISHER'S PREFACE TO SECOND EDITION

The Waltz of the Shadows was Magda Herzberger's first book of what we now view as a trilogy driven by her experiences during World War II and her suffering at the hands of the Nazi's. The second is her phenomenal autobiography, *Survival*, which readers have called the most compelling memoir of the Holocaust ever written. The third is a children's book, *Tales of the Magic Forest*, filled with stories that inspire and teach young people about life—its joys and its dangers.

We started 1st World Library because we believe that it is critical that all society's stories and messages have the chance to reach their audience and that this can not happen if we have to depend solely on the traditional publishing industry. This trilogy is our finest example, probably the main reason we were compelled to publish books.

Working with Magda and Eugene Herzberger has been one of the finest experiences of our publishing career. Being part of bringing this trilogy to the world is a blessing beyond measure..

As Magda said in her comments to this edition, *The Waltz of the Shadows* is being presented exactly as it was twenty-two years ago, except with the addition of two poems and two associated musical compositions, *Prayer for Assistance* and *Requiem*. These two works were both written after the publication of *The Waltz of the Shadows*, but we believe strongly that they must be a part of this second edition.

Brad Fregger
Barbara Foley
1st World Library, Inc. Austin, Texas
January, 2006

TABLE OF CONTENTS

ACKNOWLEDGMENTS

The poems listed below originally appeared in the sources cited:

"The Battlefield," published in *Across U.S.A.*, by Manitou Publishing Co., Sioux Falls, South Dakota.

"Bondage," published in *United Poets*, Summer 1974, by The American Poets Fellowship Society, Charleston, Illinois.

"Boundless," published in *Life Is Tremendous*, 1972, by Imperial Publishing Co., Winnipeg, Manitoba, Canada.

"Consolation," published in *United Poets*, Fall 1973, by The American Poets Fellowship Society, Charleston, Illinois.

"Daybreak (To My Husband)," published in *El Viento*, Autumn 1973, by Valley Publications, Huntington, West Virginia.

"Epitaph," published in *The Gift*, 1973, Northwoods Press, Bigfork, Minnesota.

"Fortune Teller," published in *Melody of the Muse*, 1973, by Young Publications, Appalachia, Virginia.

"Fumbling in the Dark," published in *The American Poet*, Winter 1974, by The American Poets Fellowship Society, Charleston, Illinois.

"I Saw Them All," published in *Major Poets*, Fall 1974, No. 26, by Pierson Mettler Associates, Hot Springs National Park, Arkansas.

"Joy of Life (To My Son)," published in *El Viento*, Spring 1973, by Valley Publications, Huntington, West Virginia.

"The Lakeside," published in *Major Poets*, Spring 1973, by Pierson Mettler Associates, Tremont, Illinois.

"Last Rites," published in *Outstanding Contemporary Poetry*, 1973, by Pied-Piper Press, Sandwich, Illinois.

"Life without Liberty," published in *Yearbook of Modern Poetry*, 1972, by Young Publications, Appalachia, Virginia.

"Nightmare!" published in *New World Action*, 1974, New World Press, Tampa, Florida.

"The Old Pear Tree," published in *Poetry Is for People*, 1972, by Mason City Banner Times, Mason City, Illinois.

"Out of Tune," published in *Shore Poetry* Anthology, The Shore Publishing Co., Milwaukee, Wisconsin.

"Prayer," published in *Year Book 1974-1975*, by the Woman's Club of Monroe, Monroe, Wisconsin.

"Resurrection (To My Husband)," published in *Lyrics of Love*, 1972, by Young Publications, Appalachia, Virginia.

"A Song Is Born," published in *Prairie Poet*, 1974, by The American Poets Fellowship Society, Charleston, Illinois.

"Suspended in Space," published in *The Fellowship Poetry Book*, 1974, by The American Poets Fellowship Society, Charleston, Illinois.

"Sweet Serenade of Summer," published in *Poetry Is for People*, 1972, by Mason City Banner Times, Mason City, Illinois.

"Triumph," published in *The Magic Ring*, 1973, by Northwoods Press, Bigfork, Minnesota.

"War," published in *The Birth of Day*, 1972, Keels & Co. Publishers, Lubbock, Texas.

"Mystery" was 2nd prize winner, Magdalena Douglas Literary Contest, Wisconsin First District Federation of Women's Clubs.

I

INTRODUCTION

REQUIEM

My eyes shed drops of tears
Into the pools of years
For those I loved and lost
And like a haunting ghost
My spirit roams around
Searching for their unknown
Burial ground —

They were the victims
Of their faith,
Sentenced to death
Without a sin,
For worshipping
The only God
They believed in —

They died without protest,
With no rebellion,
Together with the rest
Of six million
Innocent Jews
In the Nazi camps
Of Germany —

3

O, Lord, please help me
To keep alive their memory —
They died in vain,
I witnessed their agony
And pain,
I heard their cries,
O, Lord, our God
Open for them
The gates of Paradise —
Let their souls
Rest in peace — — —
Forgive mankind's atrocities — — —

BONDAGE

Lost in the mountains of past memories,
And trapped in the high elevations of emotions,
I climb the rough boulders of illusions,
And chase the mirages of haunting dreams —
I follow the winding streams of thoughts,
Caught in the wilderness
Of petrified reminiscences —
And, almost losing my senses,
I look around for a trace of hope
But I find only bare rocks,
A hard ground,
And a lonely world without a sound
To which I am forever bound.

THE WALTZ OF THE SHADOWS

It was a cold night,
Near the end of December.
Winter's white messenger,
Filled with rage and anger,
Was circling wildly
Above the deserted and lonely streets,
Blowing its frozen stars all over
And rattling the windows and doors
Of the silent homes ...
I was sitting in my favorite armchair,
Listening to the monotonous
Rhythmic sound of the gas heater ...
Gradually I got lost
In the world of thoughts ...
My mind was soaring
On the wings of phantasy ...
Suddenly I heard the Grandfather clock
Striking the midnight hour,
And a feeling of strange apprehension
Descended upon me,
Thinking that this may be the time
When the spirits rise
From their secret hiding places
To haunt and surprise the living ...
Roaming freely everywhere,
Opening door locks,

6

Lifting heavy bolts,
And peeking through the darkness
Into the lighted rooms ...
There is no barrier for the soul ...
I looked behind,
But I couldn't see spirits around.
There was no movement, no sound ...
Then all at once
The memory of a dreadful experience
Invaded my mind ...
I recalled my despair,
My sufferance and agony ...
The shadows of the past
Were creeping slowly into my room
To increase my doom ...
I could sense their presence ...
I heard a haunting melody ...
But there was no one in sight ...
Shivers were running down my spine
From fright ...
The tune of an old waltz
And the sound of sliding feet
Reached my ears ...
Invisible spectres were dancing around me
    The "Mad Waltz of Memory" ...
The music grew louder and louder,
I wondered if it would ever cease ...
I shouted, "Go Away, Go Away, Please!"
But the shadows couldn't be barred —
For my aching heart
They had no regard.
Finally, gathering all my strength,
I yelled:
"Who do you think you are?
You have no right to intrude
Upon my privacy!"
The music stopped abruptly.

The silence was followed
By moments of suspense.
I became very tense.
The shadows were approaching me ...
They came nearer and nearer.
I couldn't see any faces —
I could detect only quiet whispers
And footsteps ...
Then a vague silhouette
From the crowd
Stepped forward.
A voice like a shattering noise
Addressed me with poise:
    "I am Fate —
    My power is great.
    I can stir up love or hate
    Bringing you joy or sorrow.
    I am the owner of Yesterday,
    Today, and Tomorrow.
    You blamed me
    For your unjust slavery
    In the concentration camps
    Of Germany ..."

    "Fate, I know you well.
    I am still in your grip.
    You are holding me
    Under your spell.
    Where were you
    When I was forcibly taken
    To that strange land?
    Why didn't you extend to me
    Your helping hand?
    You didn't listen to my call.
    You let me fall, after all ..."

    "My ungrateful friend,
    May I introduce you to

My steady companions:
'Hunger', 'Thirst', and 'Misery'?
You've met them before
In the extermination camps
Of Germany ..."

The room filled up
With sighs and moans,
And three indistinct forms
Were facing me.
One by one,
They stepped forward,
Introducing themselves
Properly:
    "We are the accomplices of Fate.
    We dwell behind the gate of hate."

    "My name is Misery.
    My nickname: 'The Dread of Everybody'.
    I am shunned and despised.
    My real face is often disguised.
    I kept you close company
    In the camps of Germany.
    You could not get rid of me
    Until you were set free ..."

    "I am Hunger —
    Do you remember me?
    During the war
    I was very busy.
    I put up my large tents
    And my trapping nets
    In the concentration camps
    Of Germany.
    I followed you
    Through Auschwitz, Bremen,
    And Bergen-Belsen ..."

"I am Thirst —
Worse than Hunger.
I was merciless.
Inflicting painful wounds
On your tongue,
Driving you close to madness.
I tortured your friends,
Your fellow prisoners,
And your family.
I kept you in slavery
Throughout your captivity ..."

"Go away, all of you!
Please leave me alone!
I remember! I remember
When you reduced me
To only skin and bone."

A sudden laughter
Echoed through the room ...
I was on the edge of doom.
Who is mocking me,
Ignoring my torture and pain,
Hammering insults
Into my tired brain?

"I am Death —
I carry disease and decay
On my breath.
You are but a Mortal
Struggling in vain.
Your strife is senseless to me.
I collect the fruits of life.
You are a helpless victim
In my power.
You will be mine
At the end

10

Of your last hour.
I harvest freely
At all times.
I am the terror
Of the poor
And of the emperor.
I don't make any exception,
I despise help or protection.
Remember me well —
No one can escape
My spell.
I spared you in Germany.
But sooner or later
You will come with me ..."

"Death, I remember you well.
All your terrible deeds
Are engraved in my soul.
You robbed me
Of those I loved.
You injured my heart,
Tearing me apart
From my family.
My lips were sealed,
But I was saved by God.
My open wounds were healed —
The pain subsided
But a scar was left behind
To remind me and Mankind
Of your cruelty.
And now, please retreat into the past,
Let my weary soul and body rest."

As I finished my last sentence,
A peaceful, soothing melody
Filtered its way
Into my room,

Chasing away
My undesired company.
I wondered who this next visitor
Could be?
A calm and soft voice
  Addressed me kindly —
    "I am Hope,
    The best friend of Life,
    Your constant guide —
    I was always at your side
    In Germany,
    Protecting you
    From the harsh blows of Fate,
    And from the flames of Hate.
    I took good care of you,
    Giving you faith, courage,
    And moral strength
    To fight despair.
    Have trust in me.
    My vigilance will never end,
    You can rely on my helping hand.
    No matter how bleak
    The scene of life may be,
    My streak of light
    Will always be in sight
    To brighten your destiny ..."

I opened my eyes —
Dawn's purple glow
Hit my window.
The birth of a new day
Was announced.
The shadows were gone
Before the rising sun
Took its place
In the sky.
I was alone ...

12

Tears were running down my face.
I was dazed, confused and perplexed,
Wondering if the shadows
Would ever return —
But I knew that they would
Once they'd found their way,
And each night from now on
With me they will stay ...

II
WAR

FORTUNE TELLER

The sorcerer's evil eye
Sees in future's crystal ball
The damnation of the soul ...
Demons, in their dark attire,
Filled with foul and sick desire,
Whirl in a wild dance
Around the burning pyre
Where the spirit is on fire ...
And after the red flames expire
Only the cold ashes remain
For the devil's domain ...

WAR

War! Master of terror!
Hide your ugly face,
Don't ever come back to our place!
Your sins shall never give you rest!
You are the killer
Who tore away children
From the mother's breast,
Slaying with your right hand,
Smashing with your left.
Your crimes I will never forget.
You! Who destroyed mankind,
Leaving tears, miseries, fright, sorrows,
Empty ruined homes, widows, behind.
You! The carrier of pest and distress,
Who cast your black shadow once upon us,
Covering, shutting out lights, thus,
Sharpen your ears,
Open your senses,
Listen to my curses:
I wish your death.
Your home should be Hell,
Burn in its fires!
Hear, Oh hear, you cruel wrath,
These are my true desires.
But I know, all is in vain.
Today you die,
Tomorrow, you are born again.

THE BATTLEFIELD

"There is the enemy —
Aim and shoot!"
Gained a small victory,
Lost a foot,
Here and there
An empty boot.
"Kill and loot!
Thrust the knife
Into pulsating life!
Carry the wounded,
Let the blood flow
On the battlefield ..."
      For what cause
      (Can be debated)
      Should you yield
      To cruelty, madness
      And hatred?
      For ambition?
      For pride?
      Or for a mistake
      You are trying to hide?
One hundred forty-six dead.
So they said.
And a single grave
For the hero, for the brave.
Whose face
Are you trying to save?

I SAW THEM ALL

I saw the flags
Of mortal sin
Wherever I have been —
I saw the flood
Of human blood
Rising on the green —
I saw the flag
Of victory
Shining in the sun —
I saw the graves
Of all of those
Who eternally
Were gone —

PLEA FOR PEACE

Come, Winter,
With your ice and snow,
Spread your white blanket
Wherever you go —

Cover the shivering grass,
The naked branches,
Fill the abandoned trenches,
Bring peace, silence, purity —

Don't let blood stain
The weary, battered earth,
Give birth to friendship,
Love, and unity —

III

PERSECUTION

THE YELLOW STAR

With tight lips
We had to bear
Our humiliation —
Upon our chests
We had to wear
The yellow star
Of discrimination —
So that everyone could see
From far
The stamp of our religion —
We were avoided
Like the plague —
In the eyes of the wicked
We were a disgrace
To the human race —
The cancer of society
Destined to be excised
From the face of the earth —
We were accused to be the cause
Of all the ills,
Pain and misery
Of the country we lived in —
Our sin was our belief in God,
Our guilt was our passion

For harmony —
We were condemned
To annihilation
Without justice, mercy, or pity —
Compassion and love
Were dead —
Hatred and cruelty
Ruled instead —
This is the story
Of the yellow star —
The prelude
To the mad ambitions
Of an insane barbarian —
To hide the truth,
To contaminate with lies
The heart of youth,
And to sentence to death
Six millions
Of innocent Jews ...

ON THE WAY TO THE GRAVE

We were hauled
Into the somber freight cars
And placed behind bars —
Then, the doors were locked —
Our freedom was taken —
We were left in the darkness
Doomed and forsaken —
Ready to be shipped
To our place of execution ...
    The slow puffing
    Of the steam engine
    Grew faster and faster,
    As the locomotive
    Pulled us further and further
    Into the unknown —
    As the train rolled on and on,
    Our last spark of hope was gone ...
        Some of us cried —
        Others tried to rebel,
        In vain —
        Sorrow and pain
        Crept into our hearts,
        Chilling our bodies,
        Clouding our minds,

27

But gradually
Most of us succumbed
To the strong power
Of destiny ...
Sitting silently,
Hour after hour
On the cold, wooden floor —
Lamenting no more —
Only a few
Were still pounding
The heavy door
With their fists,
And shouting, "Open up!
Why are we here?"
No one could hear
Our desperate outcry ...
Then suddenly
The train stopped —
We were in Germany,
Facing the barbed wire fence
Of Auschwitz ...
Humiliated, heartbroken,
Waiting for the judgment
Of guilt
To be pronounced
On the innocent ...
Each of us
Was possessed by fear,
We were so near
To death
That we could feel
Its breath.
We were robbed, trapped,
And with horror,
Into the German concentration camps
We stepped!

IV

THE
CONCENTRATION
CAMPS

AUSCHWITZ

MEMORIAL

Death was lurking constantly
In the concentration camps
Of Germany.
So many times
I could have been selected
For the gas chambers
To meet the horrible fate
Of all the infants, the children,
The young, the old,
The sick, the disabled,
Who were executed
In the mysterious
"White House" of Auschwitz,
Whose naked bodies were thrown
To the furnaces
Of the huge crematoriums,
Whose ashes were used
On the fields and the gardens.
Day and night
The great flames
Of the ovens
Belched from the chimneys.
The air was filled
With the strange,

Sickening, sweetish odor
Of burning flesh.
I mourn you, innocent victims,
Members of my family,
My fellow prisoners,
Who were silenced forever
By the Nazis.
Your wailing cries
And your terrible contortions
Met deaf ears
And blind eyes.
I was destined to live,
To bear my misery.
God chose me to return,
To remind the world
Of your agony.
Erecting tombstones
In your memory —

HOLOCAUST

Clad in rags
In the midst
Of the German concentration camps
In Auschwitz,
I addressed, in my despair,
An SS guard
Carrying in his truck
A tank of fresh water —

> "A drop of water, I implore
> And nothing more!
> Each day on my tongue
> New wounds burst,
> I am dying of thirst —"

My fellow prisoners
Who shared my misery
Were crying out loudly —

> "Water, water, please,
> Our sores we want to appease,
> We are dying of thirst!
> Have pity on us!
> Our tortures must cease!"

But our voices hit the hard stones,
Our bitter outcry
Met only cruelty —
The SS guard reached
For his thick and heavy
Rubber stick briskly
And started beating us savagely —
The harsh blows
Cracked the skin on our backs —
We were bleeding,
Revealing the bare human flesh —

"Get out of my way!"
He shouted.
"I don't care if you live or die —
From this water
You will have no share!
Blows I can give you plenty,
So don't provoke me!"

He placed his foot
On the gas pedal
And speeded up his vehicle,
Leaving everyone
With painful, ugly scars —
Some of us were raging,
Our parched lips were craving
For water —
Those who tried to follow his truck
In order to catch the moisture
From the exhaust pipes
And the few drops
Dripping from the small opening
Of the shaking tank
Were savagely massacred
By the rolling tires —
The driver was madly running over
Their emaciated bodies

With that heavy monster of his —
Finally, he left
And I looked at death's
Horrible aftermath
Stretched out in my path.
I let out a cry
In the silent
Chambers of my soul:
　　　　"Oh God, don't let us die!
　　　　What became of human dignity?
　　　　Where are the limits of cruelty?
　　　　Has kindness become unknown?
　　　　Are history's barbarians
　　　　Rising from their graves? —
　　　　To bring disaster and slaughter?
　　　　Oh, where are you, Justice?
　　　　Come on your wings
　　　　And save us from the gutter
　　　　Of hatred, crime, and prejudice.
　　　　Chase away these human deformities
　　　　And bring us decency.
　　　　Grant us peace!
　　　　Oh, God, don't turn away from us!
　　　　Upon you I call.
　　　　Almighty ruler of the universe,
　　　　Don't let us fall.
　　　　Give us strength to bear
　　　　All this humiliation
　　　　And degradation.
　　　　Let your people survive
　　　　The trials of torture
　　　　And extermination —
　　　　I pray for myself,
　　　　For my family,
　　　　And for my fellow prisoners —
　　　　Oh, Lord, send us hope and courage.
　　　　Don't let us stagger.
　　　　Don't let death

Thrust into our hearts
Its poisoned dagger —
Send us courage
To control our fears,
And hope, to wipe our tears —
Grant us faith to fight
And to ignore the pain —
Almighty God, guide us well —
Don't let us sink
Into sorrow's deep well!''

NIGHTMARE!

Behind thick clouds
Of false illusion
Dwell the phantoms
Of delusion,
Spreading chaos and confusion
Over the distorted world below,
Letting their tears of madness
Flow
Amidst a weird creation
Of wild fancy and imagination ...

It is raining in my heart.
Drops of sadness fall
Upon my sick and suffering soul
Drowning my joy ...

I crumble like an old
Discarded toy ...

For sanity I pray
While my spirit turns slowly
Dull and gray ...

DELUSION

I am lying in my bed,
Feeling a dullness in my head ...
Somebody cries.
I open my eyes ...
I feel a sharp pain
In my chest ...
A stranger is boring a hole
In my breast ...
Reaching for my heart
To tear it apart ...
Leaving in its place
An empty space ...
With horror, I realize
That my hands and feet are tied
And all my movements are denied ...
I try to shout for help
But no sound leaves my throat,
My vocal cords are caught
And squeezed by terror ...
Fresh blood is staining
The pure color
Of my sheet ...
Then, I see a white hand
Wiping everything clean,

And there is no trace of me
Or of the place
Where once I have been ...
Could this be real?
Or is it a fake?
Am I dreaming?
Or am I awake?

CRY FOR HELP

Oh, my soul,
Upon you I call
In my unhappy moments.
Bring consolation,
Ease my torments —
Help me to find
Peace and contentment.
Lead me to your happy shore,
Apply your healing balm,
Cure my sore,
Keep me alive and warm
To be able to resist
With stoicism and heroism
Life's tortures which persist.
Send to me
The spirit of Euphrosyne,
To revive my joy and optimism.

CONSOLATION

Gentle Zephyr,
Be speedy on your way,
Don't let the summer fade away ...
Cool its burning cheeks,
And wipe its streaks of sweat,
And let the blue sky
Reflect its flawless hue
On the dark earth,
And lift on your wings
The heavy sigh
Of the spirit.
Bring relief to the sufferer
Who helpless, like a falling leaf
In Autumn's grip
Asks your help,
And strip the dark shadows
Of the soul,
Don't let grief
Take its toll ...

BREMEN

THE STREETS OF BREMEN

We were five hundred
Jewish prisoners,
Women with lost identity,
Captives of the Nazis,
Transferred from Auschwitz
To the port of Bremen,
To clear the ruins
And the charred bodies
From the devastated streets
Of that doomed city.
We were in the sharp claws
Of the cruel SS guards.
They afflicted us
With insults and blows.
They tortured us with hunger,
Thirst and misery.
We were exposed to hard labor,
Condemned to unjust slavery,
Forced to carry
The heavy remains
Of the shattered buildings
And destined to be annihilated
After our last drops of strength
Were extracted.

Wearing wooden Dutch shoes,
Our feet wrapped in rags,
We dragged ourselves
Through the deep snow.
Icy winds freely cut their pathways
Through our lightly covered
Shivering bodies.
We were tired, weak, and weary;
Yet, we maintained our faith
And pride,
Waiting for the Allied Forces
To set us free.
The dark clouds of tragedy
Were hanging over the forsaken city.
I felt sorry for humanity.
The earth was shaking,
Bombs were exploding,
Funnels of black smoke
Were twisting in the air,
Poisoning the atmosphere.
I remember a young girl
Caught by the fire,
Fleeing from her burning home.
Her slender body was trembling
From fear and pain.
She was crying desperately,
"Please save my family —
They are trapped inside".
But all efforts of rescue
Were in vain.
Encircled by the raging flames
Her house was rapidly collapsing
To the ground —
Her parents were never found.
She wasn't the only victim
Of the war.
I have seen so many more
During my captivity

In the second largest haven
Of Germany.
Daily, caravans of German citizens
Were moving away,
Seeking refuge,
But we had to stay
And bear with dignity
Our solemn destiny;
We were marked for death
And stripped of liberty,
While the world and mankind
Were robbed of beauty,
Peace, and harmony —

FUTILITY

A frail and feeble old woman
Was digging a hole —
Poor soul!
Her face was wrinkled,
Her skin looked shriveled,
Her spine was bent,
Her hair lost its color and shine,
It was as white as snow
At Christmas time.
She wore a pair of old brown shoes.
A shabby grey coat
Covered her thin body.
A wornout black velvet hat
Trimmed with purple lilies
Rested on her head,
Reminding me
Of a faded funeral bouquet.
Her knotty fingers
Were grasping firmly
A small shovel,
Plunging it continuously
Into the hard ground.
She kept on working frantically,
Gasping for air

Now and then
In despair —
As I watched her,
My heart was filled
With compassion and pity.
I asked her kindly,
        "Dear Lady,
        What are you looking for?
        Please save your energy,
        Don't work so hard anymore."
She straightened, and looked at me.
Her eyes were dull and sad.
Tears ran down her pale cheeks,
And pointing to the piles of crumbled ruins,
She said,
        "This is what's left
        Of my house —
        There is buried my family.
        I am looking for my silver box
        Containing my golden jewelry.
        I could sell it,
        And get some money
        So I could eat
        A few warm meals occasionally,
        And I could have a bed
        To rest my aching bones.
        To hell with wars!"
She shouted —
And she grabbed again her instrument,
Thrusting it deeper and deeper
Into the earth,
Hunting for her lost treasure
And hoping to find the small remains
Of a lifetime —
But the hole was empty and hollow,
Lost was the past, the present,
And the tomorrow —
I turned to her and exclaimed,

"Please tell me your name,
You and I
Share a common destiny,
We both are caught
In war's ugly, cruel
And bloody game —"

TRIUMPH

Death celebrates
Its victory,
Marching wildly
Through the city,
Striking the young
And the old,
Beheading life
On its cold scaffold —
Then, leaving behind
A severed mankind
Ridden with pain and agony,
The cruel spectre retreats
To its kingdom
Of earth and stone,
Mounting its throne
Of human bone,
Waiting to launch
The next assault
On its constant enemy,
The live, pulsating body ...

BERGEN-BELSEN

ANGUISH

In the silence of the night,
My heart is filled
With sorrow and fright.
I am wide awake,
Repeating over and over,
"Why didn't I escape?"
I am a victim
Of persecution,
Locked in this horror camp
Of execution,
Destined to perish
By starvation.

I am falling slowly
Into a mental stupor,
What am I guilty of?
My crime is my religion,
My faith in God
And my belief
In love and compassion.

In the hands of the SS monsters
Is my fate —
O, Lord, give me strength

57

To bear the strain,
Don't let my mind disintegrate —
Help me restore
The broken pieces
Of my shattered life,
Cure my sore,
Ease my pain,
Liberate me
From the devil's domain.

I feel so weary, so strange ...
King of the Universe,
Only you can change
My destiny.
Please listen to my laments,
Hear my cry,
And don't let me die —

FORLORN

At my journey's end
In this mortal land,
I sink into time,
Like footprints
In the dunes of sand —
I fight in vain
Like a bird in a cage —
My trace is swept
By the winds of age —
I am free to live,
But not for long —
To eternity
I can never belong —
And yet, when death
Summons me to captivity,
I beg and struggle for life,
Hour after hour,
Before I yield
To its inevitable, absolute,
And invincible power ...

SOLITUDE

In the doorway of death
The lights stay shut
And the ties of life are cut —
No rays of hope penetrate
The thick walls
Where doom and silence falls —
No distant cries and calls
Are passing through
To stir the failing hearts
Which once were new.

UNEXPECTED VISITOR

Two knocks upon my door ...
Short tappings on the floor ...
A faint call
Across the hall ...
I tumble and fall ...
Invisible hands
Lead me in a trance
Of no return ...
Thoughts, passions, actions burn ...
Memories fade ...
My fate I can't evade ...
My life is at stake ...
I shatter, and then break ...
My time is up, no mistake —

LAST RITES

There is a funeral
In the cathedral
Of my soul ...
The bells toll
Their sinister tune,
And the solemn sound echoes
Through the grief-stricken shadows ...
The tall candles are lighted
While the cherubs of peace
Circle around unsighted ...
And by the pale flames
Death plays its old games ...
Only the spirit is free
Escaping the doomed body
Rising above time and age
Standing on life's stage
Defying finality ...

LIBERATION

The putrid and sickening odor
Of decaying bodies
Fills my nostrils —
I lie on the bare ground
Next to the high piles
Of stripped naked
Decomposing corpses
In the midst of the German
Extermination camps
Of Bergen-Belsen,
Waiting to die —
I watch the walking skeletons
Passing me by;
They are my fellow prisoners —
I listen to their cries,
Their sunken eyes
Resemble mine.
We are the innocent victims
Of the mad demons
Of history.
I feel the cold touch
Of the gaping earth below,
And I know
That soon I will go

To join my dead companions
And all those I loved and lost —
Soon, into eternal darkness,
I will be tossed.
I look up to the blue sky,
Saying, "Goodbye" to life,
Asking in desperation:
"Why are we condemned unjustly
To torture, to death,
To starvation?"
We are punished
For our faith in God
And for being a part
Of the Hebrew generation.

The old birch tree
Next to me
Is witnessing my agony.
With my thin shriveled arms
I struggle to embrace
The wrinkled trunk
Of my silent friend,
Whispering faintly:
"Come Death, and take me".

But suddenly a warm current
Is passing through my body,
I see the bright light of Life
Chasing away the dark night
Of Oblivion,
Saving me from Death's pavilion.
A loud voice hits my ears:
"Drop your frights and fears,
We defeated Germany!
We are British fighting soldiers
Bringing you the news of victory!
YOU ARE FREE!"

I see the advancing
Heavy British tanks,
And to God I say my thanks —
Then I look around,
My eyes follow
The sick, the dying, and the dead
Stretched out on the hard ground.
My heart fills up
With awe and sorrow —
Many of us were struck and crushed
By the unkind hand of fate.
For them, the bells of Victory
Ring too late.
And others, like me,
Who survived,
Will mourn forever
All those left behind ...

DEPARTURE

After my liberation
I spent six months
In Bergen-Belsen,
Recovering slowly
From the harmful effects
Of starvation.
During this period of waiting
And desolation,
I would walk daily
To the nearby birch forest
In search of peace
And consolation.
The tall slender trees
Listened so often to my cry,
Witnessing my loneliness.
There I would express
My gratitude to God
For not letting me die.
Surrounded by the beauty
Of His creation
I found solace
And a few moments
Of joy and happiness
In my isolation.

Then, one day I was ready
To return to my native country,
Hoping to find survivors
In my family,
Beseeching the Lord
To grant me courage,
Strength and tenacity
To face reality.
With deep sorrow
I left behind
Those I loved and lost,
And all the innocent victims
Of persecution,
To follow my unknown destiny
With the "Ghost of Memory".

V

RETURN

SABBATH LIGHTS
(to my Mother)

Every Friday night
My mother would pray
By the candlelight ...
I remember her slim figure;
Her shiny black hair
Was lightly covered
With a dainty lace;
She wore a happy smile
On her pretty face.
In a soft voice,
With closed eyes,
She uttered slowly
Her words of benediction:
> *Blessed art Thou,*
> *O, Lord, our God,*
> *King of the Universe,*
> *Who has sanctified us*
> *By Thy laws*
> *And commanded us*
> *To kindle*
> *The Sabbath light*
Then, she kissed me,
And my father,

71

With affection —
I saw the white bread
And the red wine
On the table.
The plates, the glasses,
And the silverware
Were neatly spread
On the handstitched cloth.
I looked at my parents,
Feeling such a deep love for both.
I was only seventeen years old,
But I knew by then
That love is more precious
Than diamonds or gold.

I saw my mother
Two years later ...
Still lighting the candles
Each Friday night.
But tears and sorrow
Shadowed our weekly ritual —
We'd learned my father had died
During his captivity
In the extermination camps
Of Germany.

And now, so many years later,
I have a family of my own
With children who are fully grown.
My mother still lights
The candles in her home,
          But she is all alone ...

EULOGY
(in the memory of my Father)

My dear father,
You left us forever ...
You had a heart of gold,
You were kind and clever ...
Why didn't you survive?
I am heartbroken, but alive —
Back from the German
Concentration camps —
But you are buried there ...
I will mourn you forever.
Why were you treated so brutally?
Only because you were a Jew.
What was our sin?
Our religion.
We were condemned
To persecution.
Your last words
Still ring in my ears
After so many years —
"My child, my dear daughter,
Soon we will be separated
From each other.
I may never return —
Be strong, don't cry.

73

Let the candle of hope burn
In your heart —
Take care of your mother,
Cherish and respect her —
Don't forget your loving father —
Remember to follow
The broad countless streets
Of knowledge,
And beware the dark
Narrow alleys
Of ignorance —
Practice the art of love,
Forgiveness, and tolerance ...''
Father, my dear father,
I can never forget you —
Your words are deeply carved
Into my memory.
Beloved father,
Rest peacefully ...

WOUNDED

I walk in pain
Through memory lane
With the fragments
Of past painful passages
Piercing my brain —

As the hours pass
I roam aimlessly
On the pavement, on the grass,
Until the night
Dims my sight —

Darkness covers my thoughts,
But my heart burns with fever
And lights up the dark sky,
Will I ever recover,
Or, will I die? —

IN YOUR MEMORY

Many years ago
A wise man told me:

"Wherever you go
My thoughts will follow —
When pain will grab your soul
Or sorrow squeeze your heart,
Think of me,
And you will never fall apart ...
My love for you
Will never die —
I may be soaring above
In the blue kingdom of the sky,
My body may be sealed
Beneath the earth,
But remember,
I shared and witnessed your birth —
I will never desert you —
I'll watch over you
When you are awake or asleep
I will listen to your voice,
I'll weep when you suffer
And laugh when you rejoice."

"O wise man
I know you speak the truth —

I left the border of youth
Standing on the stage of maturity,
Wearing the gray signs
And the dry lines of age —
I understand now
All the teachings
You bestowed upon me
Through the years —
Since you left me,
My eyes shed countless drops of tears —
My dear father,
How can I thank you
For all the years of love,
Wisdom, guidance and care —
How can I ever bear
Your absence —
I always feel your presence —
For me you never died —
I see you in my dreams,
Floating on life's streams —
You are here with me,
We never are apart,
Death could never tear you out of my heart —
Wherever your mortal body rests
May be death's domain —
But your spirit will always remain
Buried within me —

My dear father,
Wherever you may be,
Under the cold rocks,
Or behind a shining star,
I am with you
Wherever you are —
My thoughts will hold forever your image —
And in my eternal pilgrimage,
My quest to reach your soul
Will be my highest goal —"

OUT OF TUNE

Like a false melody
Painful to the sensitive ear,
So are the dissonant sounds
Of a dying passion
Coming near ...
Distorted, disjointed,
Yet still alive,
Played over and over
By the untuned violins of the heart
With no end
But a start ...
Until the strings break
And fall apart.

MEMORIES

In the white room
With the grand piano
I listened to a solo.
I watched the fingers
Move rapidly
From right to left,
From left to right.
Hitting the white
And black keys
Firmly.
It was my aunt
Playing.

The room was filled
With music,
And images
Started moving
In front of me:

A river, with its gentle ripples,
A quiet summer afternoon,
With birds chirping
And crickets singing,
Here and there

A butterfly,
Blooming flowers
Stretching their stems
And turning their heads
Toward the sky ...
I saw the cat
Through the window,
Passing the hollow
Old oak
With its shabby cloak;
The dog barked
And chased his enemy away ...

I wish I could stay
Once more
In the house
Of my grandparents,
And meet again
All the friendly tenants
Of the yard:

The orchard,
The flowers,
The grass,
The tall Linden trees;
To hear again
The buzzing
Of the bees;
To relive
The happy memories,
And the curiosity
Of the child ...

Farewell
To all of these,
But they still live
In the hidden corners
Of the past
Where they will
Forever last.

THE OLD PEAR TREE

I still remember the old pear tree
Standing majestically
In my grandparents' yard
At the time
When I was a small child.
I was playing with my cousins in the room.
Suddenly, we flew out of the house fast
Like a witch on a broom.
We shook the old tree violently,
Waiting for its fruits to fall, impatiently.
We picked up the big pears quickly,
Examining each one separately,
Admiring their giant size,
Uttering shrieks of surprise.
The good old tree
Delivered us yearly
Its produce faithfully.
We looked up at it with pride,
Saying loudly:
      "Here is the best friend
      Of grandmother's yard."
It still echoes in my ears,
Our laughter mixed with tears,
After so many years.

FUMBLING IN THE DARK

Dark silent night,
Display your bright
Celestial ornament
On the distant firmament.
Illuminate my sight,
Help me find my way
In the obscure future.
Don't let me stray away
From the right direction
Let me traverse
The serene peaceful section
Of the eternal universe —

HYMN OF GRATITUDE

Wake up my friend,
Be thankful
That you are alive —
Respect the Creator's omnipotency —
Come, and pray with me
To be bestowed
With good health,
With luck and happiness —
Cherish and caress
Each precious moment
Given to you by God.
Inhale life's sweet fragrance —
Cling to the present
As long as you can —
Bow with humility
To the inevitable fate
Of man —

RESCUE

Don't fear the devil
If your conscience is clean
For in its evil kingdom
I have been ...
I was taken there by force!
The flames of hatred and cruelty
Were burning around me,
But I put up my shield
Of faith, hope, and love,
Given to me from above,
And no hot tongues could reach
My spirit or body ...
The raging fire was extinguished
By the will of God ...
I was set free,
To return to life — to continue my strife,
But, I was told,
"Never let vengeance get hold
Of your soul —
No sin should be your goal".
I listened, and decided to forgive,

For all the injustice, pain, and grief
That once was poured upon me,
Upon my people,
Upon my family,
And tried to live
With peace and harmony —

VI

RESURRECTION

DAYBREAK
(to my Husband)

Come, my love
The night is gone —
Yesterday slipped away
On the Milky Way —
And the purple dawn put on
Its sapphire crown
Ushering the new day
And making way
For the rising sun —
Let us resume
Our daily course
On life's terrain —
Let the returning light
Illuminate our sight
And start a new episode —
Let us decipher a part
Of the hidden code
Of creation
On our temporary
Earthly station.

CONTEMPLATION

Reality is pounding in vain
The heavy doors
Of the haunted chambers
Of phantasy,
Where, entangled in the fine
Intricate webs of imagination,
The mind is a captive
Of endless time —
The loud outside call
Doesn't reach the intellect.
The doors are locked tightly,
And controlled
By an invisible power,
Releasing the latch
Only at a certain hour.
In those deep, silent compartments,
Void of sounds and action,
Takes place the resurrection
Of the soul,
While the inner self
Is kept in seclusion,
In a world of illusion.

YEARNING

Light a star
And show my way —
I have come from far,
Don't send me away —
I passed through
Dark and dreary years,
Shedding pools
Of bitter tears —
I am weak and weary
And covered with mud —
Almightly God,
Please open for me
The ports of true poetry
And let me enter
The enchanted land
Of the bard —
Take my hand
And lead me
To the colorful gardens
Of phantasy,
Where the flowers of
Imagination bloom —
Let their sweet fragrance
Charm my heart —

Let my spirit be subdued
By the eternal force of creation,
And be carried
Through the secret
Passages of life,
Where the songs
Of the universe
Are chanted —
Let my thoughts wander
Through the ancient
Sacred shrines
Of the written verse —
Let my mind explore
The mystical realm
Of rhythm and rhyme —
Let me be the chime
Of time,
Emitting the broken sounds
Of a forgotten century —

JOY OF LIFE
(to my Son)

In the depth of the forest I rest
In the silent nest
Of solitude
Where beauty dwells
Casting its magic spells
Upon my soul —
The rustling leaves hum
Their haunting melody
And the dark earth
Displays the treasures of life —
Each moment is filled
With ecstasy —
I try to capture
All that my eyes can see
Forgetting age and mortality
Singing the song of eternity —

PASTORALE
(to my Daughter)

Sing for me
The songs of life
Hum the gentle melody
Of heaven, earth and sea ...
Play for me the mellow notes
Of nature's symphony ...
Touch the strings of my heart.
Music will start to flow
Into my blood
And it will flood
My spirit and body
With beauty, peace and harmony ...
Let me be the instrument
Of eternity
Striking the keys
Of serenity ...

A SONG IS BORN

My harp lies still
Waiting for swift fingers
And melodies to fill ...
There in the corner
Behind the rocking chair,
It longs to be taken out
Into the fresh air,
Where the rabbits sleep,
Sheltered in their lair,
Where the birds sing
Their songs of spring and summer,
Where the woodpeckers hammer ...

When nature's sounds
Are put together,
A song is born
On the strings of my harp,
And thus is recorded
The song of the lark,
The whisper of the grass,
The whistle of the wind,
The bouncing of raindrops
Hitting the treetops,
The strong beat

Of heaven's drummer,
The breath of spring,
The pulse of summer.

Come, my harp
Let's go outside
This room is small
The world is wide ...

SWEET SERENADE OF SUMMER

The wind is whistling
    High above,
Its passionate song
    Of love.
The tune is traveling
Through the clouds
    Fast,
Reaching the earth
    At last.

Nature is put
In a trance;
The trees begin
To dance.
Swaying their numerous arms,
Clapping their leafy palms,
The river swings
In undulating curves,
Flowers lean
To each other.

The air is filled
With the sweet serenade
    Of summer.

THE LAKESIDE

When the silence is broken
By cheers and laughter,
The sunshine looks brighter;
The water seems softer —

Empty boats and canoes
Are swaying
Waiting for sailing —

In a side corner,
Humble and shy,
Wrapped in yellow ruffles,
Covered with droplets of dew,
And surrounded by a few
Tall weeping willows,
A lonely lily slumbers
On soft green round pillows
Under the blue sky,

While the warm breeze
Of summer
Is humming an old lullaby —

WILL YOU STILL LOVE ME?
(to my Husband)

Will you still love me
When I grow old and gray?
Will you still recall
The young girl
You carried away
As your bride
On a rainy day
In Fall?
Will you still hold me tight
Like on our wedding night?
Or, will you forget
The first day we met
In Summer
When roses were blooming
And birds were singing?
Will our cheerful laughter
Still be ringing in your ears?
Will you still remember
All the happy years
We spent together?
Please, keep the glowing light
In your heart, for me, forever —

RESURRECTION

(to my Husband)

Bury me
Under the old willow tree ...
With dry earth
Cover me ...
Place then the tombstone ...
I will remain alone
Dead flesh and bone ...
Come back sometime later
In my place
You will find a red flower ...
Pick me up
Take me home
Place me in the fresh, cool water ...
Let me live again with you
For a few more days ...
Then, throw me away
When my petals and stem
Will decay ...

VII

A SEARCH
FOR FREEDOM
— THE PROMISED
LAND

LIFE WITHOUT LIBERTY

Life without liberty
Is plain agony.
Day after day, no changes.
The days pass one after the other
Always in the same manner.
Nothing is good or bad,
Monotony slowly drives you mad.

But that's life, full of convention.
                              Reality
Never comes to our attention;
At the end of our days
We don't achieve
                              immortality.
The struggle goes on and on
Until one day we depart,
With regret, with fright.
Darkness and solitude
Is our price.
Such a high price
                              to give
For a hard life
                              to live.

A SEARCH FOR FREEDOM
— THE PROMISED LAND

We were the slaves
Of destiny,
The prisoners of war,
Locked in the cells
Of history —
We were humiliated,
And robbed of liberty —
But one day,
We were set free —
We looked for the promised land.
We swore that our search for freedom
Would never end —
We crossed the rough sea
And navigated through
The turbulent ocean
To come to this country,
To join democracy —
We took the oath
Of loyalty,
And we became
The truthful citizens
Of this great country —
We belong to a free nation,
And finally,
We have the opportunity
To live with peace and harmony ...

SUSPENDED IN SPACE

High up here
On the mountain top
Facing the sky,
No other sound I hear
But the loud cry
Of the wind,
And the hard knocks
Of the falling rocks —
The cold blocks of stone
Shelter my loneliness —
Enwrapped in stillness
And surrounded by grandeur
And beauty,
I feel no pain,
No strain.
No thoughts of futility
Cross my mind.
I left behind
The twisted, restless world
With all the follies
Of mankind,
To offer my soul
To infinity.

BOUNDLESS

Poet, rise above the earth,
Leave your place of birth,
Let your spirit explore
The universe.
Like a searching, lonely pioneer,
Make your rounds
In the heights,
Stop your fights,
Let the pressure
Of the atmosphere
Push away your earthly bounds —
Cling to the boundless wings
Of your imagination —
Touch what you can't see
Sense what you can't touch —
Release the latch of phantasy,
Withstand the strong current,
And try to catch a fleeting moment
In the air.
Then, let its contour imprint itself
Into your palm,
To be the record
Of a forgotten memory —
Poet look down

In the midst of your journey.
And read the flashing message
Projected to you
From below
Which says:

      "Nothing forever stays —
      Bathe in the bright rays,
      But at sunset
      The darkness will carry you down.

      From here you started,
      Here, you will return,
      When your lights
      Will stop
      To burn —"

MYSTERY

Somewhere, at the edge of nowhere,
Upon the unpaved road of the future,
The silhouette of my fate is projected ...
But my mortal eyes can't see
The shape of my destiny ...
Nor can my spirit grasp
Life's unpredictable course of action ...
Only my striving body
Feels the agony of pain
And the joy of resurrection ...
I am but a wave
In the ocean of existence
Driven by the current of my thoughts
And protected by God's assistance ...

EPITAPH

Look for my verse
In the archives of time,
Turning the battered
Yellow pages of old rhyme.
Although you never saw my face
Nor ever heard my name,
We still belong to the same
Invisible Power
Who destines our first
And last hour.
Friend of my spirit, be kind,
Read my song —
I am but a shadow
Of the past,
Leaving behind
Only a track of words.
Please follow my lines,
Don't let them die —
Once I was also alive,
Filled with passion and drive,
Living with beauty by my side.
I rejoiced and cried,
And tried to reveal
The hidden wonders of life

Till the end of my strife —
Some day, when the cold
Eternal night
Will extinguish your flame
And cover forever your sight,
Encounter we might —

PRAYER

Almighty God,
Upon you I call.
Don't let evil spirits
Possess my soul —
Don't let hatred
Strangle my love,
Or despair
Crush my hope —
Tie me with the rope
Of patience
To the pillar of strength
When anger erupts
In my mind —
Don't let emotion
Blind my reason —
Teach me the psalm
Of faith
And restore my calm —
Dispel my doubts and fears
While the bells of life
Toll my years —
Let the warm rays
Of affection and compassion
Conquer my spirit —

O, Lord, our God,
Please disperse
The seeds of peace
And brotherhood
Upon the earth,
As time rolls
On the wheels
Of the universe —

MUSIC FOR PRAYER

PRAYER
For Baritone Solo and Piano
With Optional SATB Chorus

Arranged by
Frank Metis

Words and Music by
MAGDA HERZBERGER

2

4

Don't let e-mo-tion blind my rea - son. Teach

unis. Teach Mm

unis. Teach Mm

me the psalm of faith, and re-store my calm. Dis-pel my

me the psalm of faith, and re-store my calm. Dis-pel my

me the psalm of faith, and re-store my calm. Dis-pel my

6

8

PRAYER FOR ASSISTANCE

Oh, God, my Creator,
Help me to play the role of peace
In life's theatre.
O Lord of the Earth
And of the firmament,
Let me represent
The Spirits of love and harmony.
Teach me honesty and decency.
Instruct me in the art of modesty.
Assist me to create my psalms
Glorifying Your Name.
Anoint me with Thy healing balms
And soothe the wounds
Of painful emotions
With Your miraculous potions.
Comfort my aching heart
And let me start a new episode
On life's station,
Perform on me the great miracle
Of Regeneration.

MUSIC FOR PRAYER FOR ASSISTANCE

PRAYER FOR ASSISTANCE
For Solo and S.A.T.B. Chorus

Arranged by
Frank Metis

Words and Music by
Magda Herzberger

Prayer for Assistance

D Profoundly, with some motion

REQUIEM

My eyes shed drops of tears
Into the pools of years
For those I loved and lost
And like a haunting ghost
My spirit roams around
Searching for their unknown
Burial ground—

They were the victims
Of their faith,
Sentenced to death
Without a sin,
For worshipping
The only God
They believed in—

They died without protest,
With no rebellion,
Together with the rest
Of six million
Innocent Jews
In the Nazi camps
Of Germany—

O, Lord, please help me
To keep alive their memory—
They died in vain,
I witnessed their agony
And pain,
I heard their cries,
O, Lord, our God
Open for them
The gates of Paradise—
Let their souls
Rest in peace ...
Forgive mankind's atrocities ...

MUSIC FOR REQUIEM

REQUIEM
They Died in Vain
For Soprano and Baritone Solo
with SATB Chorus and Piano Accompaniment

Arranged by
Frank Metis

Words and Music by
Magda Herzberger

A Sadly, with some motion

eyes shed drops of tears in - to the pools of years For

eyes shed drops of tears in - to the pools of years For

mp

those I loved and lost, and like a haunt - ing ghost, My

those I loved and lost, and like a haunt - ing ghost, My

mf

My

mf

My

Requiem

B Mod. slow, march-like ♩ = 80

ground. _____ They were the vic - tims of their faith,

ground. _____ They were the vic - tims of their faith,

ground. _____ They were the vic - tims of their faith,

ground. _____ They were the vic - tims of their faith,

Sen - tenced to death with - out a sin, For wor - ship-ping the on - ly God

Sen - tenced to death with - out a sin, For wor - ship-ping the on - ly God

Sen - tenced to death with - out a sin, For wor - ship-ping the on - ly God

Sen - tenced to death with - out a sin, For wor - ship-ping the on - ly God

4

Requiem

Requiem

8

14

Slowly and mournfully

They were the vic - tims of their faith.

They were the vic - tims of their faith.

They were the vic - tims of their faith, They

They were the vic - tims of their faith, They

With - out a sin, for

With - out a sin, for

died in vain.

died in vain.

16

They   died   in   vain.

They   died   in   vain.

ABOUT THE AUTHOR

Magda Herzberger was born and raised in the city of Cluj, Romania. She is a poet, lecturer, composer, and the author of six previously published books: the first and second hardcover editions of *The Waltz of the Shadows, Eyewitness to Holocaust, Will You Still Love Me?, Songs of Life*, and her most recent work, *Survival*, the compelling autobiography of Magda's early life in Romania and her suffering at the hands of the Nazis.

The Waltz of the Shadows is the second book in Magda's "Holocaust Trilogy," the first book is *Survival*, and the third is a children's book, *Tales of the Magic Forest*, filled with wonderful stories which reflect the valuable lessons she learned during those terrible years.

Magda was a marathon runner, skier, and mountain climber. She and her husband, Dr. Eugene Herzberger, a retired neurosurgeon, reside in Fountain Hills, Arizona. They have a daughter Monica, a son Henry, and two grandchildren.

Magda's primary goals are to instill love for poetry in the hearts of people through her work, to keep the memory of the Holocaust alive, and to show the beauty of life through her writings and music. Her philosophy of life: Have faith, hope, and love in your heart—believe in impossible dreams and make them come true—cherish each moment of life—and never take anything for granted.

1st World Library (DBA Groundbreaking Press), publisher of the hardcover version of this Second Edition of *The Waltz of the Shadows* and *Survival*, also publishes, an inspiring book of Magda's prayers, *Devotional Poetry*, and, coming soon, another book of her poetry, *If You Truly Love Me*, and her first children's book, the afore mentioned, *Tales of the Magic Forest*.

Magda may be contacted at the following email address:
Magdaherzberger@yahoo.com